I0139841

# ECHOES
# OF
# ANOTHER
# MAN

*Mia McCullough*

**BROADWAY PLAY PUBLISHING INC**
New York
www.broadwayplaypublishing.com
info@broadwayplaypublishing.com

ECHOES OF ANOTHER MAN
© Copyright 2008 by Mia McCullough

All rights reserved. This work is fully protected under the copyright laws of the United States of America. No part of this publication may be photocopied, reproduced, stored in a retrieval system, or transmitted, in any form or by any means, electronic, mechanical, recording, or otherwise, without the prior permission of the publisher. Additional copies of this play are available from the publisher.

Written permission is required for live performance of any sort. This includes readings, cuttings, scenes, and excerpts. For amateur and stock performances, please contact Broadway Play Publishing Inc. For all other rights contact The Susan Gurman Agency.

Cover photo & image design by Johnny Knight
First printing: February 2008
I S B N: 978-0-88145-373-7
Book design: Marie Donovan
Word processing: Microsoft Word
Typographic controls: Ventura Publisher
Typeface: Palatino
Printed and bound in the U S A

ECHOES OF ANOTHER MAN was developed in part through Stage Left Theater's Down Stage Left development program, American Theater Company's Relatives reading series, and through Chicago Dramatists.

ECHOES OF ANOTHER MAN was originally produced by Actor's Express in Atlanta, GA; (Jasson Minadakis, Artistic Director; Kristin Hathaway-Hansen, Managing Director), opening on 6 January 2005. The cast and creative contributors were:

THE PATIENT . . . . . . . . . . . . . . . . . . . . . . . . Daniel May
KATIE . . . . . . . . . . . . . . . . . . . . . . . . . . . Kate Donadio
DOCTOR PARK . . . . . . . . . . . . . . . . . . . . . . Addae Moon
IRIS . . . . . . . . . . . . . . . . . . . . . . . . . . . . .Tracey Copeland
RAINA . . . . . . . . . . . . . . . . . . . . . . . . . .Shannon Eubanks

Director . . . . . . . . . . . . . . . . . . . . . . . . . Jasson Minadakis
Set design . . . . . . . . . . . . . . . . . . . . . . . . .Rochelle Barker
Costume design . . . . . . . . . . . . . . . . . . . . . . . Jamie Bullins
Charge scenic painter . . . . . . . . . . . . . . . . Amy Ferguson
Dramaturg . . . . . . . . . . . . . . . . . . . . . . . Michelle Johnson
Lighting/Sound design . . . . . . . . . Joseph P Monaghan III
Technical director . . . . . . . . . . . . . . . . . . . .Casey Johnson
Stage manager . . . . . . . . . . . . . . . . . . . . . . . Rita A Marcec

The Chicago premiere of ECHOES OF ANOTHER MAN was at Stage Left Theater (Kevin Heckman, Producing Artistic Director). The cast and creative contributors were:

THE PATIENT ..................... Cory Krebsbach
KATIE ................................ Cat Dean
DOCTOR PARK ..................... Keith Uchima
IRIS ............................ Demetria Thomas
RAINA ................... Marguerite Hammersley

*Director* .......................... Kevin Heckman
*Scenic design* ......................... Dustin Efird
*Costume design* ..................... Jana Anderson
*Sound design* .................... Christopher Fuller
*Stage management* ..................... Liz Dunker
*Lighting design* ....................... Julie Ballard

# CHARACTERS & SETTING

THE PATIENT, *a white man in his early thirties, trim and fit*

IRIS, *a nurse, Haitian, mid twenties to mid thirties*

KATIE, *a young widow, early thirties*

RAINA, *the manager of a famous artist, very proper and insecure, forties*

DOCTOR PARK, *a surgeon at his peak, late thirties, early forties*

ORDERLIES, *two non-speaking roles, appearing in a couple of hospital scenes and helping with scene changes.*

*Time: the not-so-distant future*

*Setting:*

ACT ONE, *a hospital room*

ACT TWO, *the Hammond living room, a street in Paris, a hospital room*

# ACT ONE

## Scene 1

*(Lights up on a hospital room and the hallway outside.
A PATIENT lays in bed, unconscious, his head wrapped in
bandages. He is fit and in his early thirties. KATIE, a woman
of similar age, enters furtively, looking behind her. As she
turns and sees the PATIENT, she stops dead, overcome. She
wears a visitor's security clearance badge around her neck.
She approaches slowly. She gently pokes him in the arm.
He does not move. She prods him more vigorously. Nothing.
After a hesitation, she takes up his hand and tries to pull
a gold band off his finger. The longer she tugs, the more
desperate she becomes. Occasionally she checks the door
to be sure no one is coming.)*

KATIE: Come on come on come on. *(She licks his finger
and tries again.)* Jesus. This is ridiculous.

*(KATIE pulls a bottle of lotion out of her purse. She squeezes
some onto the PATIENT's hand and tries again. She pulls the
ring off and collapses into a chair. His hand dangles off the
edge of the bed.)*

KATIE: *(To PATIENT)* This was not a good idea.

*(KATIE laughs for a moment, then her mood shifts abruptly.
She gets a shiver, a bad one. She shakes it off. She looks
around the room [not at the PATIENT].)*

KATIE: Steve?
God, it's like I can feel your breath on my neck.

(KATIE *stares at the* PATIENT *a moment, then takes up his hand. She gently rubs the back of his hand against her cheek. Suddenly the he squeezes her hand and opens his eyes with a gasp. She screams, dropping his hand.*)

KATIE: Oh shit, shit, SHIT!

(KATIE *dashes out of the room. The* PATIENT *eyes close again as the lights fade.*)

## Scene 2

(DOCTOR PARK *enters the darkened hospital room. He checks the patient's vitals on all the monitors, then looks at the* PATIENT's *eyes with a pen light.*)

DOCTOR PARK: Hi, Steve. Sorry. Claude. (*He pulls up a chair and sits. Long pause. He looks at the* PATIENT, *then looks away and says:*) Please don't die on me. (*He takes a bottle of Pepto Bismol out of his coat pocket and swigs some. Then several beats.*) I should have gone into research.

(*The lights fade.*)

## Scene 3

(*Lights up on the hospital room.* DOCTOR PARK *is asleep in the chair next to the comatose* PATIENT. IRIS *enters, turns on the light, sees* DOCTOR PARK *and smiles.* DOCTOR PARK *does not stir. She goes around and checks all the monitors.*)

IRIS: Good morning, Doctor Park.

DOCTOR PARK: Hmm? What? Oh. Iris.

IRIS: You should go home to sleep. Your wife cannot be happy about this vigil.

DOCTOR PARK: He's got to go one way or the other, sometime in the next couple of days. He can't stay like this indefinitely.

IRIS: Of course he can.

DOCTOR PARK: Don't try to make me feel better, Iris.

IRIS: If you want some breakfast, you should ask someone to get it for you: the T V people have permanently set up camp in the cafeteria. Oh, and the venerable Doctor Park the First has been spotted in that vicinity.

DOCTOR PARK: Dear old Dad.

IRIS: He is very proud, telling all the reporters who he is.

DOCTOR PARK: And all about his own surgical pioneering no doubt. He just likes talking to the press. *(A sigh)* At least he doesn't have clearance to get on the ward.

IRIS: *(To the* PATIENT*) Bon jour,* Monsieur. How are you this morning? A little sun, I think. You are looking too pale. *(She opens the curtains.)* And a lovely view of the protesters.

DOCTOR PARK: You know they were chanting "mutilator" at me when I came in yesterday. And you wonder why I don't go home.

IRIS: There are plenty of other people calling you a pioneer and a genius.

DOCTOR PARK: So, it balances out, is that what you're saying?

IRIS: It keeps your head from getting so big.
   Anyhow, some of them have a valid point of view.

DOCTOR PARK: What part of it is valid?

IRIS: He clearly did not care for himself well.

DOCTOR PARK: *(With humor)* You're in no position to make that judgment.

IRIS: His diabetes had progressed excessively for a man his age: his kidneys were gone, his leg, his sight—

DOCTOR PARK: The disease progresses differently in different peop—

IRIS: You have heard the stories. You just don't want to acknowledge them because you got the match you were looking for.

DOCTOR PARK: I can assign someone else to his primary care if you're not comfortable—

IRIS: I am fine. I am only playing devil's advocate. The protestors are silly with their chanting and their signs, but their opinion is justified.

DOCTOR PARK: *(Carefully)* You think the religious fanatics out there are justified, too?

IRIS: I believe some important questions have not been asked about the conse/quences.

DOCTOR PARK: /Like what?

IRIS: Now is not the appropriate time to have this conversation, Doctor Park. It is too late.

*(*DOCTOR PARK *closes the curtains. Beat)*

DOCTOR PARK: I heard a rumor.

*(Beat)*

IRIS: You should not listen to hospital rumors.

DOCTOR PARK: I heard you requested a transfer to maternity.

IRIS: I filled out the papers. I've not submitted them.

DOCTOR PARK: We would miss you, Iris. You're the best nurse we've got up here.

IRIS: I know.

(RAINA *steps into the doorway holding a garish painting. She wears a laminated security pass around her neck.*)

RAINA: Good morning.

DOCTOR PARK: Ms van den Hoven.

RAINA: How is he?

IRIS: The same.

DOCTOR PARK: What's that you have there?

RAINA: I brought one of his paintings. I thought it would be good to have something familiar when he wakes up. Since I can't be here.

DOCTOR PARK: Yes, well, I'm afraid we can't have that in here just yet. As you know, we'll be studying his memory very closely. We won't want to introduce familiar objects for several days after he comes out of his coma. You do understand.

RAINA: I do. I just—

DOCTOR PARK: I know, it's difficult to wait. But when we do start trying to trigger his memory, some paintings would be perfect. You, of course, know which pieces would be best.

(RAINA *nods. A beat*)

RAINA: Will you be introducing Claude to his paintings before you introduce him to...people?

DOCTOR PARK: Yes, I believe that's how we have it scheduled.

RAINA: *If* he wakes up.

*(Beat.*

DOCTOR PARK: Yes.

RAINA: Is it all right if I talk to him now?

DOCTOR PARK: Oh. Well. Yes. But if he wakes, you should leave the room immediately, as we've discussed.

RAINA: Yes, you've been very clear on that point.

DOCTOR PARK: I have an interview with the morning news people. I'll be back to check in later. *(He exits.)*

RAINA: I know they have to study him, as he recovers, but it seems awfully cruel to keep him away from everything familiar. He won't even recognize himself. Won't he be terrified?

IRIS: I will do all that I can to make sure he is comfortable.

*(Beat)*

RAINA: Are you Haitian?

*(Beat)*

IRIS: Why does it matter where I am from?

RAINA: I just wondered if perhaps you spoke French. It was Claude's first language. He might find it easier when he wakes up.

IRIS: I will keep that in mind.

RAINA: Could you give us a moment?

IRIS: ...Yes. I will be outside.

*(IRIS exits leaving RAINA alone with the PATIENT. She goes to the bed and looks at him a long moment.)*

RAINA: Hi. It's me.
  Claude?
  Please don't stay in a coma forever. I hate this place.
*(Pause)*
  I still can't believe you're really in there.
  I miss your face.
  Not that there's anything wrong with this face.
It's fine. I just....

(RAINA *sits in the chair next to him, not looking at him.*
*After a moment she takes his hand in hers. She looks at it.*
*It feels wrong. She puts it back on the bed.)*

RAINA: I don't even know what color your *eyes* are now.

(RAINA *reaches towards his face, pulls back, thinks about it,*
*and then gently pulls open an eyelid. She lets go and sits*
*again.)*

RAINA: Hazel.

*(Lights fade.)*

### Scene 4

*(It is night. The lights come up on the* PATIENT *and* DOCTOR
PARK *asleep in the chair beside him. The* PATIENT *is wide*
*awake and is staring at his hand, trying to get his fingers to*
*move. They do, ever so slightly.* DOCTOR PARK *stirs, sees the*
PATIENT.)

DOCTOR PARK: Oh. Oh. You're awake. SHIT you're
awake. Can you see me? *(He waves his hand in front of the*
PATIENT's *face.)* Can you hear me? Do you understand
me?

*(The* PATIENT *is alarmed. Clearly he can see, though maybe*
*not well.* DOCTOR PARK *flashes his penlight in the*
PATIENT's *eyes.)*

DOCTOR PARK: I'm sorry. I'm sorry. I'm not trying to
scare you. I'm your doctor. Doctor Park. You may not
remember me.

*(DOCTOR PARK moves his finger back and forth in front of*
*the* PATIENT's *face.)*

DOCTOR PARK: Can you follow my finger?
    Good, good. I know you probably can't see that well.
It'll take your brain a little while to remember. Can you
squeeze my hand?

(DOCTOR PARK *does some reflex tests on the* PATIENT. *He is giddy with excitement. The* PATIENT *still looks alarmed.*)

DOCTOR PARK: Ah! You moved your toe! You moved you toe!

You probably won't remember how to speak right away. I don't want you to worry about that. You may not even understand what I'm saying.

But you're awake. And that...that is amazing. Thank you. Thank you for being awake. I've... I've got some people who are going to want to see you.

(DOCTOR PARK *runs out, leaving the* PATIENT *confused. Lights fade.*)

## Scene 5

(*It is morning. The* PATIENT *is awake and is looking around the room.* IRIS *walks in with a tray of food.*)

IRIS: *Bon jour, Monsieur. Comment allez-vous?* Your assignment for today is to remember how to eat and drink. What do you think about oatmeal?

(IRIS *offers the* PATIENT *a spoonful of oatmeal. He looks at it blankly. She lets out an exasperated sigh and recites:*)

IRIS: Your name is Claude Lescure. You are fifty-three years old and you are an artist. Your body was deteriorating and quickly approaching the end stages of diabetes. Your brain was transplanted into the body of a thirty-two year old professional golfer in a vegetative state. You are now awake and in your seventeenth day of recovery. My name is Iris, and I am your nurse. Would you like some oatmeal? (*She stares at him a moment and then, with another sigh, repeats it in French.*) *Vous vous appelez Claude Lescure. Vous avez cinquante-trois ans et vous êtes artiste. Votre cervelle a été transplantée dans le corps d'un joueur de golfe professionel ayant trente-deux ans et étant en état végétatif. Vous êtes courramment éveilé et cela est votre dix-septime jour de récupération. Je m'appelle Iris, et je suis votre infirmière. Voudriez-vous de la bouillie de gruau d'avoine?*

*(The* PATIENT *shows no sign of understanding.)*

IRIS: Doctor Park keeps telling me you don't understand a word we say, but I don't believe him. I don't. I think you understand me in French and in English, *oui?*

*(*IRIS *stares him down. The* PATIENT *looks away, confused and uncomfortable.)*

IRIS: Come on. Have some of this. It's oatmeal. You *eat* it.

*(The* PATIENT *sniffs it.)*

IRIS: Or smell it.

*(The* PATIENT *wrinkles his nose and pushes* IRIS*'s arm away.)*

IRIS: You don't like oatmeal, do you, Claude? You remember the smell? Well, I don't like it either. How about some juice? *(Waving a straw under his nose)* It's a straw. You suck on it. In your mouth.

*(*IRIS *puts the straw in the* PATIENT*'s mouth. He blows. The juices bubbles over.* IRIS *screams a little and then laughs so hard she can hardly speak.)*

IRIS: *Non, Monsieur*...don't blow.

*(The* PATIENT *laughs too, perhaps more with* IRIS *than at himself, as a baby would.* IRIS *finally catches her breath.)*

IRIS: You don't blow. Not *(She blows out puffs of air on his hand. Then she demonstrates the sucking inhale.)* In.

*(*IRIS *demonstrates sucking a few more times, but dissolves into laughter again. The* PATIENT *is amused.)*

IRIS: This is the first thing that everyone has to learn, Claude. The first thing you learn is to suck your mama's teat. You suck, you survive. I know this is not such a pretty package, but try.

(*The* PATIENT *stares at it blankly.*)

IRIS: Don't make me unbutton my blouse to jog your memory.

(*The* PATIENT *sucks up some juice. He is rather surprised.*)

IRIS: Now swallow it. Swallow.

(IRIS *gulps a couple of times. Juice begins to dribble out of the* PATIENT's *mouth. She wipes it up.*)

IRIS: It's okay. You're getting it. Try some more.

(*The* PATIENT *sips some more.*)

IRIS: Now, swallow!

(IRIS *presses on the* PATIENT's *throat lightly causing him to swallow reflexively.*)

IRIS: There you go! Stop the presses, he drinks! Sad thing is, they *might* stop the presses. Never seen so much fuss over one man.

All right, let's try some more.

(*Lights fade.*)


## Scene 6

(*It is fairly dark in the hospital room. The lights from the monitors glow brightly. The* PATIENT, *slowly, quietly gets out of bed. He is shaking, but can balance with some effort. He takes a few timid steps but he is tethered by the I V. He pulls off his I V. It beeps. He looks out the window. Then he shuffles over to the bathroom. The bathroom light comes on automatically as he enters. He spies himself in the mirror, at first not realizing that he is looking at himself. He looks at himself intently, touching his face, his nose, looking in his mouth. He looks inside his hospital gown*

*and stares at his body, surprised by it, slightly amused.
He is surprised by the sound of his laugh. He makes faces at
himself, testing out his voice and his facial muscles, making
simple sounds, but no words. He touches his bandages and
then buttons a couple buttons on his top. He peers out into
the hallway. Seeing no one he exits. Lights fade.)*

*(In the half-light the* ORDERLIES *escort the* PATIENT *back
into bed. He is dejected, like a child told to come in and play.
The* ORDERLIES *put him in restraints.)*

## Scene 7

*(It is morning. The* PATIENT *is awake and is looking around
the room. He tugs at his restraints, annoyed, trying to
scratch an itch on his head.* IRIS *enters. She is amused.)*

IRIS: *Bon jour, Monsieur. Comment allez-vous?* ...Still not
talking, eh? I heard you had a little adventure last night.
Got yourself lost in the psych ward and put everyone
in a panic. Their star patient escaped. Good thing they
recognized you up there. The psych ward is the land of
no return, don't you know. *(Laughing)* Of course, even
if you tried to come back down here, the stupid security
guards probably wouldn't have let you through—
*(She wiggles her security pass at him)* —you're the only
one on the floor who doesn't have a clearance pass.
...A brilliant oversight.
  The night nurse might get fired over your *petit séjour.*
Not very nice of you.

*(The* PATIENT *tugs at his restraints while giving* IRIS *a
pleading look.)*

IRIS: No.

*(*DOCTOR PARK *enters with a couple of orderlies carrying a
cardboard box full of things, a video camera and a tripod.)*

DOCTOR PARK: Good morning, Iris. Steve. Sorry.
Claude. I need to stop doing that. Is he ready?

IRIS: I have no idea. Would you like his restraints
on or off?

(The ORDERLIES set up the camera and help prep the
PATIENT.)

DOCTOR PARK: I don't think they're necessary during
the day.

IRIS: All right. If he wanders off again, it'll be on your
head.

DOCTOR PARK: I'll take full responsibility.
   Well, Mister Lescure. I have a box of things from
your life here, to see if we can trigger your memory.
I'm going to videotape your responses. Iris, would you
set up the wireless E E G, please?

(IRIS affixes electrodes to the PATIENT's head. DOCTOR
PARK pulls a tape player out of the box. DOCTOR PARK
stands in front of the camera and very seriously addresses it.
IRIS is amused.)

DOCTOR PARK: Mister Claude Lescure, in his late teens
and twenties, before he turned to the visual arts, was a
concert pianist. I have been provided with a recording
of him playing his favorite piece.

(DOCTOR PARK pushes play. The music begins in the middle
of the piece. For a moment, the PATIENT is more focused on
the camera than on the music, but after the first few bars he
stares intently at the tape player. He points at it suddenly.
Then he looks at his hand, his fingers. The last notes are
struck. There is thunderous applause. The PATIENT tries
to bow. He holds his head, in pain.)

DOCTOR PARK: Careful, careful. Your skull is still
mending. Well, he remembers that, obviously.

(DOCTOR PARK *rests the* PATIENT *back against his pillows.*
PATIENT *inspects his hands, wiggling his fingers, mimicking
piano playing.*)

DOCTOR PARK: Okay. Let's try something else. What do
we have?

(DOCTOR PARK *pulls three well worn paint brushes out of
the box and hands them to the* PATIENT.)

DOCTOR PARK: Here you go. Do you remember these?

(*The* PATIENT *looks at them, perplexed. He swirls the bristles
against the palm of his hand. No reaction. He sniffs them.
Instantly memories are triggered: his eyes widen. He sniffs
the brushes again and is caught up in another surge of
memories. He looks around the room trying to focus,
unsure of what's happening to him.*)

DOCTOR PARK: (*To camera*) Interesting that he chooses
to sniff them since smell, of all the senses, triggers
memory most strongly. (*He waits for the* PATIENT *to
react more.*) Do you remember what those are for?

(*The* PATIENT *rubs the bristles on his tongue.* DOCTOR
PARK *grabs the brushes away from him.*)

DOCTOR PARK: No, no, no. Not in the mouth. Why
don't I take those. Let's find something else. Here's
a photo of someone you know quite well.

(DOCTOR PARK *hands the* PATIENT *a photograph. The*
PATIENT *looks at it, and after a moment he recoils. He tosses
the photo away from himself, crying out and batting at the
images before his eyes, which quickly devolves into smacking
himself in the head.* IRIS *jumps in and pins his arms to his
side.*)

IRIS: No, no, *non Monsieur. Non.* If you try to hit your
head again we're going to put you back in the restraints.

(*The* PATIENT *clings to* IRIS, *terrified.* DOCTOR PARK
*rummages through the box.*)

IRIS: Perhaps that's enough remembering for one day, Doctor Park.

DOCTOR PARK: Just one more thing, I think. *(He pulls out a half empty tube of paint and unscrews it.)*

DOCTOR PARK: Here, Claude, look at this.

*(The PATIENT still clings to IRIS, but he turns his head to DOCTOR PARK. DOCTOR PARK waves the paint under his nose.)*

DOCTOR PARK: Remember this?

IRIS: He might try to eat it.

*(The PATIENT grabs the tubes, squeezing pigment onto his hands. The ORDERLIES take the tubes as the PATIENT drops them.)*

IRIS: I don't think it's good to touch—

DOCTOR PARK: Just a minute.

*(The PATIENT searches for a surface. He smears the paint on the wall behind the bed. The ORDERLIES support him as DOCTOR PARK takes notes. The PATIENT pushes his fingers through the fresh paint on the wall, then collapses onto the bed, exhausted, breathing hard. The ORDERLIES and IRIS clean him up.)*

DOCTOR PARK: *(Addressing the camera)* Clearly the smell and the tactile sensation of the paints have triggered a rush of memories, and though the patient cannot yet speak, he still seeks to express himself through the paint. *(He turns off the camera)* Please clean his hands. That'll be all for today.

*(DOCTOR PARK exits.)*

IRIS: It's all right, Monsieur. It's all right. I see it is a lot of work, remembering who you are. I'm glad those were not oil-based paints. Housekeeping will not be pleased.

(IRIS *pulls the covers over him.* RAINA *appears in the doorway.*

RAINA: Excuse me, Iris?

IRIS: Yes? Oh, Miss, I don't think you should come in right now.

(IRIS *moves* RAINA *back out into the hallway, partially closing the door behind her.)*

RAINA: Doctor Park said he thought it would be all right.

*(Hearing* RAINA's *voice, the* PATIENT *sits up and listens.)*

IRIS: When did he say this?

RAINA: Just now. I saw him in the hallway.

*(The* PATIENT *slowly gets out of bed and goes toward* RAINA's *voice.)*

IRIS: I cannot believe—Ms van den Hoven, I don't think it's a good/ idea.

RAINA: /You can't stop me, Iris. I have his permission and it's been three weeks. No one told me I would have to wait three weeks!

IRIS: Monsieur Lescure just had a very strange reaction to seeing your picture. He was very upset.

RAINA: My picture upset him? Maybe because he doesn't know where I've been. Did you think of that?

IRIS: I don't know, it's possible.

*(During the following line, the* PATIENT *moves into* RAINA's *line of vision.)*

RAINA: How would you like to wake up in a different body, be completely disoriented—Claude!

IRIS: Oh, *Monsieur,* you should not be out of bed.

(IRIS *tries to guide the* PATIENT *back to bed, but he shrugs her off, entranced by* RAINA. *He walks to her very slowly, reaching toward her face.*)

RAINA: Claude? Is that you? Do you remember me?

(*The* PATIENT *touches* RAINA'*s face very gently. Assaulted by some violent memory, he jerks his hand away. She is a bit overcome.*)

RAINA: It's all right, Claude. You can touch me.

(RAINA *tries to take the* PATIENT'*s hand, but he pulls away and covers his face. He stumbles away from her.*)

IRIS: Careful, Claude. This way. Back to bed.

(*The* PATIENT *balls up under the covers, hiding his face.* RAINA *follows them in.*)

RAINA: Claude? Is he all right?

IRIS: Perhaps he is remembering something that frightens him.

RAINA: But why would he be— (*She steps fully into the room and sees the painting for the first time.*) Did he do this?

IRIS: Just now, when Doctor Park was testing him.

RAINA: Claude! Your first painting in your new body! Do you know how many people have already asked to buy this? And you painted it on a hospital wall! I can't sell a hospital wall. Unless they'd let me cut it out.

(*The* PATIENT *continues to hide under the covers.*)

IRIS: You are not helping, Ms van den Hoven.

RAINA: I can't believe he did this.

IRIS: You need to leave. *Right* now.

(*Beat.* RAINA *sees the* PATIENT *cowering.*)

RAINA: Claude? I'll be back tomorrow, Claude. Everything will be okay. I'll work out everything. *(She exits.)*

IRIS: *Monsieur? ...Monsieur?* It's all right. I know it must be very hard. We have asked too much from you today. I am sorry.

*(IRIS sits next to him and caresses his shoulder. Lights fade.)*

*(In the half light RAINA enters and leans several of Claude's paintings against the hospital walls. The PATIENT follows her, unseen, turning the paintings around so that they face the wall. RAINA exits and the PATIENT returns to bed.)*

## Scene 8

*(Lights up on the hospital room. IRIS enters the hospital room carrying a tray with oatmeal, juice and a banana.)*

IRIS: *Bon jour, Monsieur, comment allez-vous?* I see you have turned all your paintings around again. What's the matter? You don't like your own work?

PATIENT: Not really.

*(IRIS is momentarily shocked. She sets the tray down and gives the PATIENT a good looking over.)*

IRIS: *Parlez-vous français, aussi?*

PATIENT: *Oui.* It sounds terrible though. I can't seem to get this tongue around it.

IRIS: Interesting.

PATIENT: Irritating. This voice is so flat and provincial sounding.

IRIS: *(Turning to go)* I must get Doctor Park.

PATIENT: *(Pleading)* Please don't.
    It's so early.

*(Beat)*

IRIS: For how many days have you been able to speak?

PATIENT: A few.

IRIS: Decided to keep it to yourself?

PATIENT: I was working some things out.

IRIS: I see you have no trouble spitting out full sentences.

PATIENT: I did at first.

IRIS: You've been practicing.

PATIENT: At night. Quietly.

IRIS: Why keep it secret?

PATIENT: I was trying to minimize the poking and prodding. It was finally tapering off.

IRIS: Yes, I suspect there will be many questions, many tests today.

*(IRIS puts the PATIENT's food in front of him and checks his monitors.)*

PATIENT: Do you have to tell Doctor Park right away?

IRIS: Yes. *(Beat)* Is Ms van den Hoven aware of your progress?

PATIENT: No. ...You don't like her, do you?

IRIS: I don't know. I think I like her better than you do. *(Now that the shock has worn off, she resumes her nurses duties as she talks.)*

PATIENT: ...What makes you say that?

IRIS: Several things.

PATIENT: I have so many memories of Raina to sift through. And there are gaps, I think. It's hard to remember how I feel.

IRIS: I wouldn't think you'd have difficulty remembering how you feel about someone.

PATIENT: Well, I do.

IRIS: Do you remember who to trust?

PATIENT: I trust you.

IRIS: *(Amused)* Why?

PATIENT: I didn't know you before. There is nothing I know about you that I cannot remember.

IRIS: That does not seem like a reason to trust someone.

PATIENT: I look at Raina, at photos of other people I knew before, and I remember them. Things we did together, conversations we had, but I don't remember what they meant to me. I can remember drinking, laughing, but I don't know if I was really enjoying myself. And some things, I remember them, doing things, but I can't imagine how I did them. And then there are things I don't remember. Or I *think* I don't remember. How do I know when I have all the pieces back?

IRIS: That must be very frustrating.
  You should eat.

PATIENT: You give me too much. I've never had a big appetite.

IRIS: You have a bigger body now, you have to eat more. You've been losing weight since the surgery and Doctor Park is not pleased.

PATIENT: Where are you from?

IRIS: ...I am from Haiti.

PATIENT: Why did you pause before you answered?

IRIS: Because I don't understand why everyone must know where I am from. It makes me tired.

PATIENT: It's because you have such a beautiful accent.

IRIS: I am not susceptible to flattery.

PATIENT: When did you come over?

IRIS: When I was eight, I believe.

PATIENT: Not one of those daring escapes by boat.

IRIS: *(Brusque)* I was flown here by a Rotary Club,
so I could have surgery. I was a sickly child.

PATIENT: And then you convinced them to let your
family come, as well?

IRIS: No. Then my family conveniently disappeared
and there was no one to send me back to.

PATIENT: They abandoned you?

IRIS: Or liberated me. It depends on how you see it.

PATIENT: How *do* you see it?

IRIS: I had seven brothers and sisters, we were always
hungry. This was probably better. If I was there,
I would be poor and sick, or dead if I was really lucky.
Here I got an education. I am a professional.

PATIENT: You know, I'm an orphan, too.

IRIS: *(Terse)* I'm not an orphan. I'm an exile. It is
different. Eat.

PATIENT: It hurts when I swallow.

*(Beat)*

IRIS: That is probably from the feeding tube. I can get
you different food. Some jello?

PATIENT: The feeding tube went down my throat?

IRIS: Through your nose and down your throat, the
intubation tube for the ventilator was in your mouth.

PATIENT: I have all these aches and pains, these odd sensations, things I didn't feel a week ago. It's as if my brain is only now recognizing the skin behind my right ear, the muscles around my ribs. And I don't know if these pains are normal for this body or if they're side effects from the surgery....

IRIS: You are probably sore here and here. *(She touches his head.)* This is from the clamps they used to keep your head in place for the surgery. And of course your skull is sore, where it's mending. Also, Mister Hammond experienced some trauma in the accident that caused his brain damage, deep bruising in the muscles and the bones, so you may be feeling some residual pain from that.

PATIENT: What about this scar on my shoulder?

IRIS: It looks old. Does it hurt?

PATIENT: No.

IRIS: It is probably a childhood injury.

PATIENT: It's strange not to know.

IRIS: Maybe it is better not to know.

PATIENT: What's this strange mark on my finger? It's all discolored and pale.

IRIS: That? ...I don't know what that would—oh.

PATIENT: What?

*(Beat)*

IRIS: It is the mark from Mister Hammond's wedding ring.

PATIENT: Oh.

IRIS: Eat.

*(IRIS exits, a little unsettled. The PATIENT stares at his hand as the lights fade.)*

## Scene 9

*(In the half light before the scene begins* RAINA *returns and turns the paintings forward again. One of the hospital walls is rotated to reveal a new painting. She sets up an easel, places a blank canvas on it, and seats the* PATIENT *in front of it. She puts a paint brush in his hand and leaves.)*

*(The lights come up. The* PATIENT *looks absent-mindedly out the window.)*

*(*KATIE *appears in the doorway. She wears a security badge. She stifles a gasp and is about to turn away when the* PATIENT *sees her.)*

PATIENT: Hello.

KATIE: Hello...Mister Lescure.

PATIENT: Do we know each other?

KATIE: No. No. I've heard a lot about you. On the news. I was coming in for a procedure and I...I was curious to see how you looked. *(Beat)* I'm sorry to bother you. *(She turns to go.)*

PATIENT: You're not. As long as you don't want to poke me or prod me or ask me inane questions, I'm happy to talk with you. Come sit down.

KATIE: I couldn't.

PATIENT: Please. I'm starved for a normal conversation with someone.

KATIE: Just for a minute. I don't want to be late for my appointment. *(She enters the hospital room.)* Are all these your paintings?

PATIENT: I guess so. The ones on the walls were painted with the new hands. The ones on canvas, those are the pre-op paintings.

KATIE: They're...vivid.

PATIENT: You're very polite.

KATIE: I don't have the most sophisticated taste.
I like landscapes. Watercolors.

PATIENT: There's nothing unsophisticated about that.

*(They get caught up in a stare, KATIE searching his face
for recognition, the PATIENT inexplicably compelled by her.
She breaks the stare, and inspects the painting on the wall.)*

KATIE: What's this?

PATIENT: I'm not sure.

KATIE: You painted it and you're not sure?

PATIENT: It's just something I felt. Like something
I can't remember.

KATIE: Is there a lot you can't remember?

PATIENT: It's hard to tell. The beginning, mostly.

KATIE: The beginning of what?

PATIENT: My life.
  Won't you sit down? I'm not contagious.

KATIE: *(Laughing)* No, I... *(She sits.)*

PATIENT: Can I get you something? Water? Saltines?
Hospital juice?

*(The PATIENT presents KATIE with a sealed cup of hospital
juice. She takes it, laughing, then she dissolves into tears.)*

PATIENT: Are you all right?

KATIE: Yes, I'm fine. I'm sorry.

PATIENT: Why are you sorry?

KATIE: I'm just a little nervous. About my procedure.

PATIENT: Are you ill?

KATIE: No, no. Nothing like that.... ·

PATIENT: Have you no one to come and hold your hand through it?

*(Beat)*

KATIE: No. I don't. *(She laughs for a moment, then cries.)* I'm sorry.

*(The* PATIENT *reaches out and puts his hand on* KATIE's *wrist and suddenly they are both struck frozen. They both stare at his hand on her arm. He feels her skin, mesmerized, slowly moving his hand up her arm.* IRIS *enters with a tray of food.)*

IRIS: *Bon jour, Monsieur*—Katie!

*(*KATIE *stands bolt upright, breaking the spell.)*

KATIE: Iris. ... I'm late for my appointment. I have to go. It was nice to meet you.

*(*KATIE *rushes out.* IRIS *turns and looks at the* PATIENT.*)*

PATIENT: Do I know her?

IRIS: I don't know. You were the one running your hand up her arm.

PATIENT: It wasn't that sort of—

IRIS: Perhaps you should decide if you want to be such a womanizer in this new body of yours. You are, of course, free to do with it as you please, but it's not the sort of thing you should take for granted.

PATIENT: But I—

IRIS: And don't play coy with me, Mister Claude. I've heard about you and the lifestyle you've led. Believe me, that woman is not your type. And she is in no state to be manhandled, so you leave her be.

PATIENT: How do you know her?

IRIS: That is none of your business.

PATIENT: Was she a patient of yours? She's got one of those security passes so she can get on the ward. Is she donating an organ to someone?

IRIS: Where do you want to eat? In bed?

PATIENT: I feel as if I've seen her before. What's her name?

IRIS: If she didn't tell you, I certainly won't.

PATIENT: Do you like me, Iris? Or am I just your patient?

IRIS: You seem like a different person everyday. How can I decide if I like you if you haven't settled on a personality yet?

PATIENT: At least I'm not boring.

IRIS: No. You are not boring. Though, perhaps, not as interesting as all the protestors and camera crews would lead us to believe.

PATIENT: Oh. Yes. Them. (*He goes to the window.*) It's amazing to me, how they stand there, day in and out. Even in the rain. (*He smiles, gives a little wave.*)

IRIS: You should not encourage them.

PATIENT: Did you know, some of the protestors were burning an effigy of me the other night?

IRIS: It was not you.
  It was Doctor Park.
  That particular group has been banned from the grounds.

(*Beat*)

PATIENT: Do you suppose they're hoping I'll die?

(IRIS *watches the* PATIENT *closely now, concerned. He looks out the window.*)

IRIS: I don't know. I don't think many of them see you as a person. A news story, a celebrity, an experiment, a blasphemy.... A symbol of all that is wrong with medicine.

*(Something about the way* IRIS *says "blasphemy" makes the* PATIENT *turn and look at her.)*

PATIENT: Do you think I am any of those things?

IRIS: I think you should eat your breakfast.

*(*IRIS *exits. After a moment of staring out the window, the* PATIENT *goes to his bed, picks up his oatmeal and begins to eat.* RAINA *enters carrying a case with an electric piano keyboard inside.)*

RAINA: Jesus, Claude! You must stop painting the walls. They won't let us take them home.

*(Random memories assault the* PATIENT. *He shakes them off.)*

PATIENT: Maybe I don't want to take it home.

RAINA: So you're going to start a career in graffiti? What are you eating?

PATIENT: Oatmeal.

RAINA: Oatmeal? You hate oatmeal.

*(Throughout this conversation,* RAINA *sets up the keyboard.)*

PATIENT: I tried it. It's good.

RAINA: You hate oatmeal.

PATIENT: I don't anymore.

RAINA: You have textural issues with oatmeal.

PATIENT: Well, my new tongue doesn't have textural issues.

RAINA: Does your new tongue have textural issues with this?

(RAINA *leans over to kiss the* PATIENT. *He puts his palm against her breastbone, holding her back.)*

PATIENT: Don't. I don't.... I'm not ready.

RAINA: *(Hurt, angry)* All right. *(Beat)* I don't know what you have to be ready for. I'm the one who has to adjust to a whole new body. *(She goes back to putting the keyboard together.)*

PATIENT: What's that?

RAINA: It's a portable piano, Claude. The sound is awful, but this is all I could get in here.

PATIENT: Why did you bring it?

RAINA: You asked me to bring it.... Before the surgery you asked me to bring it. So you wouldn't get rusty. Don't you remember?

PATIENT: No. Did you bring music?

RAINA: Sheet music? I've never seen you use it.

PATIENT: I think I used it.

RAINA: I'll get some, later. Do you want to try it?

(RAINA *puts a chair in front of the piano. The* PATIENT *sits and tries to play some awkward scales as* RAINA *inspects the artwork on the walls.)*

RAINA: It's sort of raw. Unfocused. Somewhat like your other stuff, but the color.... I've never seen you blend the colors like this. Interesting, but...I suppose it'll take you time to get back into the swing of things.

*(The* PATIENT *punches the keyboard.)*

PATIENT: They're too big.

RAINA: What's too big?

PATIENT: These fingers. The tips are too fat. And they're all calloused, the keys don't feel familiar.

RAINA: The callouses will go away. You just need to practice a little.

*(The* PATIENT *tries to play another scale. His fingers stumble. He tries to work out a melody he remembers. He looks up at* RAINA *watching him.)*

PATIENT: I can't remember how to play it, I need the music. It doesn't look right with these hands.

RAINA: So try it with your eyes closed.

*(The* PATIENT *does. He tries a simple Bach piece. First one mistake. Then another. He plays slowly, out of tempo and with much effort.* RAINA *comes around behind him and gently, lovingly sets her hands on his shoulders. He gets up and moves away, repelled by her touch and what it makes him remember.)*

RAINA: You were getting it.

PATIENT: How could you want to kiss me? After everything...?

*(*RAINA *is quite taken aback. She turns to the painted wall, distracting and composing herself.)*

RAINA: I can bring you something other than canvas, if you need another surface, but please don't...paint the walls anymore. *(Pause)* Is there something else you need?

PATIENT: No.

RAINA: Different paints? Some oils?

PATIENT: Maybe watercolors.

RAINA: Watercolors?

PATIENT: Is there something wrong with that?

RAINA: No. I'll get you some paper as well, then.

PATIENT: All right.

RAINA: Would it help if I posed for you?

PATIENT: No!

RAINA: I'm repulsive to you now.

PATIENT: No! You're beautiful.

RAINA: Too old, now that you've dropped two decades?

PATIENT: No.

RAINA: I'm just not worthy of your art.

PATIENT: My art isn't worthy of you!

RAINA: Claude, you're being ridi/culous.

PATIENT: /Could you go, please? My head hurts.

RAINA: I'll get some watercolors.

(RAINA *exits. After a moment the* PATIENT *turns back to the piano. He tries to play.* DOCTOR PARK *enters and stands in the doorway, listening. He holds a golf bag full of clubs.)*

*(After several mistakes the* PATIENT *punches the keyboard.)*

DOCTOR PARK: It's frustrating.

PATIENT: My fingers won't work. I can hear the music, I can see the notes on the page, I can even visualize my fingers on the proper keys, but I can't make my hands do it. Even when I was blind I could still play.

DOCTOR PARK: It'll take some time.

PATIENT: I don't think *time* is the issue.

DOCTOR PARK: Recovery from surgery can be frustrating, but it's good to let yourself adjust. You wouldn't want to be working all at once. It would be too jarring.

PATIENT: You say that because you're not cooped up in a hospital.

DOCTOR PARK: *(Ruefully)* Aren't I? *(Long pause)* When
I was doing my residency, I hurt my hand. I...I used
to carry a scalpel in my coat pocket. The plastic cap
that covered the blade came off and the blade poked
through the fabric of my coat. I was just bringing my
hand down to my side. After gesturing, something
simple. I saw this red fluid hitting the floor in front
of me in this pulsing spray, and it took me a minute
to realize it was *my blood*.

I had some nerve damage. They did a couple of
surgeries, but they weren't sure if I'd regain full range
of motion. For a time, a couple of months, I didn't know
if I could be a surgeon anymore. Some days I wasn't
sure if I wanted to be a surgeon. I finally had an out.
A reasonable excuse.

You know, your career, your life is on this path and
you gather momentum to the point where you can't get
off the path without hurting yourself. It doesn't matter
if you're wildly successful or mediocre, you're still
a slave to that momentum. But if fate steps in and
suddenly stops everything—you slice a nerve, you
get a brain transplant—then while you're stuck there
in that place of recovery...you can either feel trapped
there, or you can take a really good look at your life
and the path you're on. Because it's not dangerous
to turn off and take another road now that you're
stopped. Recovery can be an opportunity to rediscover
yourself.... *If* you don't spend all your time being
so angry that you can't move.

PATIENT: I don't know, Doctor Park. I don't know that
this feels like much of a vacation.

DOCTOR PARK: I didn't say that. Recovery is a lot of
work. Your piano, for instance: I'm not surprised that
you can't play. When you practice something over and
over, like a piece of music, it's not only your brain at
work. There's muscle memory. Those hands don't play

because they don't remember. They don't know the
language of music. Steve Hammond didn't use the
nerve pathways from his hands to his brain for tickling
the ivories. Here. Hold this.

(DOCTOR PARK *pulls a pitching wedge out of his bag and
hands it to the* PATIENT.)

DOCTOR PARK: You ever play golf, Claude?

PATIENT: No.

DOCTOR PARK: Ever held a golf club?

PATIENT: No.

DOCTOR PARK: Not even for putt-putt?

PATIENT: No.

DOCTOR PARK: Perfect. I want you to take this club
and stand there. Pretend the ball is right here. Pretend
you're going to hit it.

(*The* PATIENT *grips the golf club in a slightly unorthodox
manner.* DOCTOR PARK *looks excited, but is containing
himself.*)

PATIENT: Am I holding it the right way?

DOCTOR PARK: Right doesn't matter. How does it feel?

PATIENT: It feels...I guess it feels...fine.

DOCTOR PARK: I should have thought to tape this.
Oh, well, never mind, just take a swing.

PATIENT: I don't know how.

DOCTOR PARK: Just try a swing. Any swing.

(*The* PATIENT *looks at* DOCTOR PARK *with much
skepticism, but then he executes a beautiful swing
and follow-through.*)

DOCTOR PARK:                          PATIENT:
That's incredible!                    Wow

*(The* PATIENT *reaches around to feel his back.)*

DOCTOR PARK: Are you all right?

PATIENT: Yeah, I...I didn't know the muscles in my back.... That was very odd.

DOCTOR PARK: Your muscles remember golf.

PATIENT: *(Joking)* Maybe I should give up painting and knock balls around, eh? Too bad I'm allergic to grass. *(He preps for another swing, waggling unconsciously.)*

DOCTOR PARK: Not anymore.

PATIENT: Oh. Yeah. I guess not.

DOCTOR PARK: God! You did it again!

PATIENT: What?

DOCTOR PARK: Look at how you're gripping the club. *(He yanks another club out of his bag and holds it in the traditional grip.)* You see, *most* people hold the club with the thumbs aligned. But Steve Hammond had an unorthodox grip, the commentators talked about it all the time. And *that's* the grip. Even the way you intertwine your fingers. It's not intuitive, it's reflexive. Isn't that amazing?

PATIENT: I guess so.

DOCTOR PARK: I've got to go get the research fellows. They'll want to see it for themselves. *(He heads for the door.)*

PATIENT: Doctor Park.

DOCTOR PARK: Yes?

PATIENT: What was he like?

DOCTOR PARK: Who?

PATIENT: Steve Hammond.

DOCTOR PARK: Oh. Well.... I'm not sure that's relevant to your/ recovery.

PATIENT: /All I know about him is that he played golf. And he was married—to his caddie, right? And he died saving a little boy from drowning.

DOCTOR PARK: Why is it important that you know him?

PATIENT: I don't know. I feel like I should. There's something disrespectful about dismissing him.

DOCTOR PARK: I think you should focus on yourself.

PATIENT: I am focusing on myself. I want to understand my physical self, and how can I do that without knowing its history?

(DOCTOR PARK *takes a moment deciding what to say.*)

DOCTOR PARK: You know, transplant recipients often suffer from survivor guilt. Or they believe that the organ they receive imbues them with some of the donors feelings or personality. It's normal, but I assure you, it's all a trick of the mind.

PATIENT: But, I'm more him than me now. The only Claude part left is several pounds of gray matter.

DOCTOR PARK: But that is the most important part. The body is just a shell, Claude. It may have the lingering muscle memory of Steve, but the presence inhabiting that shell is all you.

PATIENT: I don't know who that is, Doctor Park.

(DOCTOR PARK *takes the golf club away from the* PATIENT.)

DOCTOR PARK: Well, that's why you need to concentrate on knowing and remembering Claude. Focusing on Steve will only confuse you, right now. *(He turns to go.)*

PATIENT: So, I guess you decided you were on the right path, then? Being a surgeon.

DOCTOR PARK: ...My hand healed. My body decided for me.

(DOCTOR PARK *exits. Lights out.)*

*(In the half-light the* PATIENT *moves the keyboard to the corner. He turns the paintings to the wall again.* IRIS *enters and helps him hang long strands of twine with colorfully painted sheet music attached to them with clothes pins.)*

### Scene 10

*(Lights up on the* PATIENT *sitting at his easel, painting.* IRIS *sits in a chair by the window, in a formal, crisp, white nurses uniform. She is visibly uncomfortable. A waltz plays on a portable C D player.)*

IRIS: I hope you're almost done. I have to punch in and get to work.

PATIENT: Just a minute.

IRIS: I don't know why you made me wear this thing. I don't like how it looks on me.

PATIENT: Don't worry. It's not what you're wearing in the painting.

IRIS: What am I wearing in the painting?

PATIENT: Nothing.

IRIS: *Monsieur!*

PATIENT: Don't have an attack. It's only from here up. *(He puts his hand level with his breast bone.)*

IRIS: *Monsieur,* people will think I behaved unprofessionally.

PATIENT: Don't worry. They probably won't even recognize you. It's not so much an image of you as what you are beneath the skin.

IRIS: You don't know me that well, *Monsieur.*

PATIENT: What I guess you are, then.

*(The* PATIENT *turns the painting so she can see. In the painting* IRIS'*s hair is in wild dreads that radiate from her head and dissolve into sprays of colorful light. Her eyes are wide and intense, her skin, dark and shimmery. She exudes power.)*

IRIS: You think I am a madwoman.

PATIENT: Not a madwoman. A sorceress, maybe, with a mad gleam in her eye.

IRIS: *(Laughing)* Have I been casting spells on you?

PATIENT: You have inspired me. Do you like it?

IRIS: It is not an accurate depiction. But, yes, I like it.

PATIENT: It's my interpretation. Artistic license. I think you lead a secret life as a voodoo sorceress.

IRIS: *(Laughing)* I must punch in. And you should get into bed and rest a bit.

*(*IRIS *tries to guide the* PATIENT *to the bed, but he catches up her right hand, puts his right hand on her waist and begins to dance with her.)*

PATIENT: *Merci, mademoiselle.* For coming in early and posing.

IRIS: What are you doing?

PATIENT: I'm trying to waltz. Do you know how?

IRIS: No, and you shouldn't exert yourself.

PATIENT: But you said yourself that all these muscles are just going to waste in that hospital bed. One two three. One two three.

IRIS: *Monsieur.*

PATIENT: You know, that was the first thing I thought when they told me they'd have to amputate my leg. That I'd never dance with a woman again.

IRIS: *(Impatient) Monsieur....*

PATIENT: And now look at me! Now I'm almost...strapping. Would you call me a strapping young man, Iris?

IRIS: With a dirty *old* man lurking inside. *(He stops, lets go, deeply stung by this remark.)* What's wrong?

PATIENT: Nothing. I'm just tired.

*(The PATIENT turns off the radio. IRIS looks concerned.)*

IRIS: You should get into bed. I'll be back in a while.

*(The PATIENT gets back into bed as IRIS exits. He closes his eyes. KATIE peeks into the hospital room. She carries a worn baseball cap. She very quietly creeps in and sits in the chair next to the PATIENT's bed. She stares at him for a moment then looks around the room at the paintings. The PATIENT opens his eyes.)*

PATIENT: You're back.

KATIE: Oh. I didn't mean to wake you.

PATIENT: I don't think you did.

KATIE: How are you?

PATIENT: You didn't tell me your name. Last time.

KATIE: Iris didn't tell you?

PATIENT: Iris doesn't tell me much.

KATIE: It's Katie.

PATIENT: Nice to meet you, Katie. They tell me my name is Claude. *(He offers her his hand to shake.)*

KATIE: I know.

(KATIE *shakes it, but it is obviously a very unsettling experience for both of them, though more confusing for him. They let go. She looks away.*)

PATIENT: I feel as if I should remember you.

KATIE: No.
 You wouldn't.

PATIENT: But we have met before. Before the surgery?

KATIE: No.
 I'm just another bored housewife who spends too much time reading about you in the papers.

PATIENT: Am I still in all the papers?

KATIE: Not so much anymore. The first few days after the surgery, you were front page, but after you started talking...the articles got smaller and...closer to the obituaries.

PATIENT: Even the doctors don't seem much interested in me now that I remember most things. Only Iris comes to see me every day, and only because she has to. Well, and Raina.

KATIE: Will they let you go home soon?

PATIENT: They can't seem to decide. That's the problem with being the *first* something. They're not sure what to do with you.

KATIE: I brought you a hat.

PATIENT: A hat?

KATIE: A baseball cap. I was thinking about your scar.... Your hair hasn't grown in as much as I thought it would.

PATIENT: They keep shaving it. Easier to stick the electrodes on.

(*Beat*)

KATIE: I just thought...maybe if you wanted to cover it up.

*(The* PATIENT *takes the hat from* KATIE, *gently.)*

PATIENT: Thank you. I've never worn a baseball cap before.

KATIE: You don't have to keep it if you don't want to.

PATIENT: No. Thank you. One must never refuse gifts from strangers. *(He sniffs the hat.)*

KATIE: Does it smell bad?

PATIENT: No.

KATIE: I washed it.

PATIENT: No. No. I'm sorry. It's this new habit of mine: I sniff everything to see if it might stir something up.

KATIE: Does it?

PATIENT: This? No. It smells like laundry detergent.

*(Awkward pause.* KATIE *looks around the room.)*

PATIENT: Why do you come to see me, Katie?

KATIE: Are you having a difficult time figuring out who you are?

*(Pause)*

PATIENT: Yes.

KATIE: I, um, I lost my job recently.

PATIENT: I'm sorry to hear that.

KATIE: And my husband...left. It was kind of one fell swoop, because I worked with my husband. I was his assistant. And so when he.... I thought it was a partnership, but now that he's gone it seems like I was an assistant. The job was more about him than me. I didn't think I was one of those people who defined myself by my husband, or by my profession, but now that it's gone, he's gone...I don't know who I am anymore. I go home and the house is empty. And I have nothing to do. No one else wants me to be their...assistant. And I don't know that I want to be anyone's assistant anyway....

It's like my entire imagined future fissured and fell away before me, and now I'm standing on the edge of this chasm, and I know that my future is out there somewhere, but I have no clue what it looks like or how I'm supposed to find it, you know? How do you step off the cliff without falling? *(She looks at him.)* I'm sorry to go on like that. I just thought you might understand. I'm sure you don't.

*(KATIE looks around the room, awkwardly. The PATIENT is desperately trying to place her.)*

KATIE: Is this Iris?

PATIENT: Yes. How do you know her?

KATIE: She looks so exotic.

PATIENT: Were you a patient of hers?

KATIE: No. *(Indicating the painted sheet music)* These are pretty.

PATIENT: They're just trifles. Practicing.

KATIE: Watercolor.

PATIENT: Yes. It's a medium I've never worked with before.

KATIE: Why on sheet music?

PATIENT: Because painting it is far easier than trying to play it.

KATIE: You can't play now?

PATIENT: My new hands are not cooperating.

KATIE: I'm sorry.

PATIENT: You're not from one of the galleries, are you?

KATIE: *(Amused)* No.

PATIENT: Not the coat check girl... No. No, it doesn't feel like that.

KATIE: Like what?

PATIENT: I'm sorry. There's so much I don't remember well. I wish I could blame it all on the transplant, but some illicit substances were involved.

KATIE: *(Turning back to the sheet music)* I used to play this piece. Dvorak always makes me think of purple. I don't know why.

PATIENT: That's blue, though, isn't it?

KATIE: What?

PATIENT: That color. It's blue.

KATIE: This one? It's purple. *(Her eyes widen.)*

PATIENT: Raina keeps telling me I'm having issues with color.

KATIE: *(Suppressing her amusement)* Um, maybe you're color blind. You know, maybe *these* eyes are color blind.

PATIENT: How do I know for sure?

KATIE: I think there's some sort of test.

PATIENT: Great. More tests.

KATIE: It's just something you look at.

*(They get caught up in a stare again. KATIE breaks it.)*

PATIENT: Were you one of my piano students?

KATIE: *(With a smile)* No.
    You certainly are waiting for a lot of ghosts to come back and haunt you. *(Beat. her smile fades)* Which is ironic, really. All this time, I've been waiting for you to come and haunt me.

(RAINA *approaches the hospital room. She pauses outside when she hears* KATIE *talking.)*

KATIE: After my father died, my mother said he kept appearing all over the house, eating at the kitchen table, or doing a crossword by the fire. Just a trick of the mind, for a second.
But she wondered if he was there all the time and she was only able to see him now and then, in her peripheral vision, if the light was just right.
I keep waiting for him; my husband. *(Kindly, without blame)* I think you're holding him hostage.

RAINA: *(Entering)* What are you doing here?

KATIE: Oh. *(Seeing that it's* RAINA*)* Oh. We were just talking. Excuse me.

(KATIE *rushes out. The* PATIENT *finally gets it.)*

PATIENT: She's my wife!

RAINA: She's not your wife. She's Steve Hammond's widow. And she has no business bothering you.

PATIENT: This is my hat!

RAINA: Jesus Christ, did she give you this ratty thing? I hope she doesn't become fixated on you. We might have to get a restraining order.

PATIENT: I'm sure she just stopped by to see...what they'd done with her husband.

RAINA: What were you talking about?

PATIENT: *(Inspecting the hat)* Nothing. I don't remember.

(RAINA *spots the painting and drops her bag on the* PATIENT'*s bed. He gets up and looks out the door.)*

RAINA: Well. This is...nice.

PATIENT: It's all right.

RAINA: Did she agree to sit for you? Or did you do it from memory?

PATIENT: I asked her to sit.

RAINA: It's nice to see that you haven't lost the ability to get women to do what you want.

PATIENT: I asked, she said yes. There was no seduction involved. She complained the whole time.

RAINA: She would. Only an ignorant woman would complain about being immortalized.

PATIENT: She's not ignorant. She was tired and late for work.

RAINA: When would you like me to sit for my first post-surgery portrait?

PATIENT: I've already done one of you.

RAINA: You have? Where is it?

PATIENT: I had the night nurse put it away, I didn't want to look at it.

RAINA: You and your ridiculous self-criticism. Where is it?

PATIENT: I don't know. You don't want to see it. It's not flattering.

RAINA: None of your art is flattering, Claude. That's the point, isn't it?

PATIENT: You don't think the painting of Iris is flattering?

RAINA: ...If you want her to look like some sort of savage jungle queen, sure. I'm going to find this new painting of me.

PATIENT: I told them not to show it to you.

*(Beat)*

RAINA: I swear, Claude, you are always finding new ways to abuse me.

PATIENT: I'm sparing you.

RAINA: Why should you start now? *(Beat.)* Here. I brought more photos for you.

PATIENT: Oh. Thank you.

*(RAINA hands the PATIENT a small photo album. He flips it open.)*

PATIENT: Whose house is this?

RAINA: That's the Goldberg's, the ones who commissioned—

PATIENT: Oh, yes. The woman with the big teeth.

RAINA: Yes.

*(They share a laugh over this.)*

PATIENT: *(Looking at another photo)* This....

RAINA: I love that picture of us.

PATIENT: This is the balcony.

RAINA: What balcony?

PATIENT: I remember falling off a balcony. This is it, isn't it?

RAINA: You were very drunk.

PATIENT: I broke my collar bone.

RAINA: I don't want to talk about that night.

*(RAINA tries to flip to the next photo, but the PATIENT grabs it from her.)*

PATIENT: But this rail... This rail is high. I couldn't have fallen over it by accident. *(He looks at her)* Was I trying to kill myself?

RAINA: Why would you ask me that?

PATIENT: Was I?

RAINA: *(Closing the door)* Claude, you can't talk about these sorts of things in here.

PATIENT: So I was.

RAINA: I don't know what you were doing. I was inside.

PATIENT: How many times did I try to kill myself?

RAINA: Claude...

PATIENT: How many?

RAINA: It was never so simple as that. You would go out in the cold—drunk and without proper clothes, you wouldn't check your blood sugar unless I kept after you like a hawk, you'd go on sugar binges. All very destructive, but not outwardly suicidal.

*(The PATIENT stares at RAINA, unsure whether or not to believe her.)*

PATIENT: I remember...hurting myself. Why would a person who would do that want this surgery? It doesn't make any sense to me.

RAINA: Claude—

PATIENT: Did I agree to this or was it all your idea?

RAINA: Of course you agre/ed.

PATIENT: /I don't remember agreeing.
   I don't want you to have power of attorney anymore.

*(Beat. RAINA tries to hide her hurt.)*

RAINA: Well, of course. It's not necessary anymore.

PATIENT: No.
   Did you find the box of letters?

*(Beat)*

RAINA: Yes.

PATIENT: Were the photos in there?

RAINA: ...I brought them.

(RAINA *hands the* PATIENT *another envelope. He pulls the photos out. She looks over his shoulder.*)

RAINA: *(Knowing the answer)* That's you?

PATIENT: Yes.

RAINA: Was it taken at the orphanage?

PATIENT: I think so. I remember this yard.

RAINA: You look so forlorn in your little bow-tie.

(*The* PATIENT *looks at the next photo.*)

PATIENT: This is the concert hall at the conservatory.

RAINA: Is that your piano instructor?

PATIENT: Yes. I don't think I liked him.

RAINA: You never really talked about him. ...Are you all right?

PATIENT: I...I wish it was clearer.

RAINA: The photo?

PATIENT: *(Very frustrated)* The images in my head. It feels like watching a bad movie. The sound keeps going in and out. I see only blips of things and then they vanish. And I can't *feel* it. I feel it, but not from the inside. I wish I could smell it.

RAINA: You know, Claude, I don't think you remembered it that well, before the surgery. It was a long time ago.

PATIENT: But how could I forget my entire childhood?

RAINA: Maybe because it's better that way, sweetheart. Maybe it's good to let the brain keep some things locked away.

PATIENT: *(An accusation)* I told you things.

RAINA: Not really. Not in any detail.

PATIENT: Who then? Who would I have told?

RAINA: Most of what I know is from things you said in your sleep, and half of that is just guesses—

PATIENT: *(Grabbing her arm)* Well, then tell me!

RAINA: Ow! Claude! Let go of me!

PATIENT: I know you've lied for me, Raina. About my drinking, and my run-ins with the law. I know you've spun tales of golden yarn for the press. I *know* you've lied for me, and I know you're good at it. What I don't know is if you've lied *to* me. If you're lying to me now. I don't know! And it scares me. Do you understand?

*(The* PATIENT *releases* RAINA.*)*

RAINA: Yes. I understand. I don't know what I can say to convince you.

*(Pause.* RAINA *rubs her arm where the* PATIENT *grabbed her.)*

PATIENT: Are you all right?

RAINA: You're a lot stronger now.

PATIENT: Did I hurt you?

RAINA: I'll be all right.

PATIENT: Let me see.

RAINA: *(Backing away)* There's nothing to see.

*(The* PATIENT *approaches* RAINA *cautiously, takes her arm, strokes it.)*

PATIENT: I'm sorry.

RAINA: I know. It's all right.

*(The* PATIENT *touches* RAINA's *face, takes her hand, and then kisses her—an apology. She smiles. He pulls away.)*

PATIENT: This is how we are, isn't it?

RAINA: Yes.

*(Pause. He steps away from her, disturbed. The lights fade.)*

*(In the half-light the* PATIENT *changes into scrubs. He eyes the door nervously. He scribbles a note on a piece of sheet music and leaves it on the bed. Then he puts on the hat, grabs another piece of sheet music and exits with stealth. Lights fade to black.)*

## END OF ACT ONE

# ACT TWO

## Scene 11

*(The lights come up on the living room of the Hammond residence. It is a modest middle class home. There is a pile of unopened mail on the coffee table, some of which has fallen on the floor. Some dirty dishes sit on various surfaces. There are three large prescription bottles sitting on the coffee table as well.)*

*(DOCTOR PARK sits on the sofa looking uncomfortable, waiting. He wears a tie and blazer. After a moment he gets up and looks at a golf trophy, then a photo on the wall of Steve immediately after he's hit the ball off the tee.)*

*(KATIE enters from the back rooms. She carries the security pass, and looks a little chagrined, a little annoyed, and very tired.)*

KATIE: Here.

DOCTOR PARK: *(Gesturing to the photo)* I was there this day.

KATIE: What?

DOCTOR PARK: At the Open. I was in the gallery where he had to chip out between those trees—

KATIE: *(Smiling)* Oh that crazy birdie shot.

DOCTOR PARK: Yeah. He shook my hand.

KATIE: Oh, God, really? You were—?

DOCTOR PARK: I mean, he shook everyone's hand.

KATIE: He was so excited.
That was one of his favorite moments, I think.
*(She gets lost for a moment, looking at the photo.)*

DOCTOR PARK: You found it, then.

*(KATIE hands the pass to DOCTOR PARK.)*

KATIE: Yes, here, sorry. I should have returned it.
I didn't take it with the intention of...coming back.
I was—I didn't even realize I was wearing it until
I got home and then I had it and...

DOCTOR PARK: I think it's a liability issue—for the
hospital administrators. No one's accusing you of
anything.

KATIE: That's hard to believe when the police show
up at your door first thing in the morning.

DOCTOR PARK: We're just trying to find him.

KATIE: He's not a fugitive.

DOCTOR PARK: No. Of course not. I'm just not sure if
he's stable enough to be....
He won't live without the medication.

KATIE: I'll be sure to give it to him if he stops by.

DOCTOR PARK: And you'll call me.

KATIE: Yes.

DOCTOR PARK: With your permission, the police have
agreed to have an unmarked car outside/ in case—

KATIE: /No. No. No more people outside my house,
okay? I had three weeks of news crews and lunatics on
my front lawn, sticking microphones in my face every
time I walked out the door, every time his condition
changed, people throwing sheep brains at me and I am
DONE, okay? Done.

*(Beat)*

DOCTOR PARK: I know this has been hard on you.

KATIE: You know what, Doctor Park? I don't think
you have *any* idea.

*(KATIE stares DOCTOR PARK down for a moment.)*

DOCTOR PARK: I don't think that the hospital, that
I have expressed the appropriate gratitude for what
you've/ given us.

KATIE: /Please don't.
  The only reason I agreed to this is because I knew
it's what Steve would have wanted. He was generous
to a fault, but I'm not and I shouldn't have been.
Do you realize that my in-laws won't speak to me?
My mother-in-law told me I was going to hell and flew
back to Iowa. And the news stories about what a *gift*
I've given to medical science, everyone painting me
as some kind of sweet young widow, it makes me want
to go out and shoot puppies.

*(Pause)*

DOCTOR PARK: I just don't want your sacrifice to be for
nothing. So if he does come here, please try to convince
him to go back to the hospital.

*(KATIE does not respond. Lights fade.)*

## Scene 12

*(Lights up on the Hammond living room.* KATIE *sits on the sofa with a mug of tea, flipping through a trashy magazine. She does not look good. There are several good-sized, full cardboard boxes sitting by the door. Outside, a dog is barking.)*

*(The doorbell rings.* KATIE *looks at the door, braces herself. After a moment, she gets up to answer it. It is the* PATIENT. *He wears scrubs, slippers, and the hat* KATIE *gave him.)*

PATIENT: Hi. *(Pause)* Your neighbor's dog is very excitable.

KATIE: It's your dog. Steve's dog. My dog, I guess. He recognizes you.

PATIENT: Will he bite? If I go pet him?

KATIE: No. He might shut up, though.

*(The* PATIENT *disappears from the door way, then immediately returns.)*

PATIENT: What's his name?

KATIE: Rasputin. Raspy.

*(The* PATIENT *exits.* KATIE *leans out the door and watches him for a moment, then she goes back to the sofa, leaving the door open. After a moment the* PATIENT *reappears in the doorway.)*

PATIENT: May I come in?

KATIE: Sure. Why not.

PATIENT: Nice dog.

KATIE: Yeah. He's nice.

*(*KATIE *doesn't look at the* PATIENT.*)*

PATIENT: Why is he in the neighbor's yard?

KATIE: They offered to take him for a little while.
I think they decided I was neglecting him.

PATIENT: You don't seem surprised to see me.

KATIE: Oh, before I forget. Doctor Park said you should
take this one three times a day, this one every two
hours, and this one, well, you can read.

(KATIE *hands the* PATIENT *the pill bottles.*)

PATIENT: Doctor Park was here?

KATIE: A couple hours ago. Who's that in the car out
there?

PATIENT: Oh. That's Kyle. He's one of the protestors.
From the hospital. He offered to give me a lift.
He said he'd wait.

KATIE: How nice. It's good to know you don't plan on
hiding out here.

(*The* PATIENT *pulls out a folded piece of painted sheet music
from his waistband.*)

PATIENT: I brought you one of these. Since you seemed
to like them.

KATIE: ...Thank you.

PATIENT: May I sit? For a minute.

KATIE: Sure.

(*The* PATIENT *sits down in an armchair adjacent to the
couch.*)

KATIE: Okay, you can't sit there. Sit on the sofa.

PATIENT: (*Getting up*) Was this his/ chair?

KATIE: /Just sit on the sofa.

(*They sit for a moment in silence. The* PATIENT *looks around
the room.*)

PATIENT: Nice house.

KATIE: Thanks.

PATIENT: It's nice to be somewhere that I don't remember and yet still feels familiar, somehow.

KATIE: What does that mean?

PATIENT: I don't know. It's hard to explain. *(Pause)* Did you have a party?

KATIE: ...No, I just wasn't expecting company. *(She begins to gather plates.)*

PATIENT: You don't have to—

KATIE: No, it's rude of me. Can I get you something to drink? A soda? Some juice? Something for Kyle? *(She exits with the dishes.)*

PATIENT: *(Shouting after her)* No. I'm fine. Maybe some water for the pills? ...I only asked if you had a party because of all the empty bottles in the recycling bin outside.

*(KATIE re-enters with the water and hands it to the PATIENT.)*

PATIENT: Thank you. I didn't mean anything about the dishes.

KATIE: Why would I have a party when my husband has just died?

PATIENT: I'm sorry. I wasn't thinking. A wake?

*(KATIE sits back down. The PATIENT takes his pills.)*

KATIE: You need a body for a wake.
   We used to entertain all the time, so we had lots of booze in the house. I wanted to drink it all, so I poured it down the sink. That's why the bottles.

PATIENT: You must be very depressed.

KATIE: Did you come here for something?

PATIENT: ...I wanted to know if you had any clothes that you wouldn't mind loaning me. I'm trying to avoid stores. My face has been on the news a lot.

KATIE: Those boxes. I packed up all his things. Take whatever you want. Take it all.

*(The* PATIENT *goes over to a box and pulls it open. He rummages through, pulling things out.)*

PATIENT: Are you going to tell Doctor Park I was here?

KATIE: After you leave.

PATIENT: You're not going to call him now?

KATIE: Do you *want* me to call him now? Would you like to speak with him?

PATIENT: No.

KATIE: You're a big boy. You can go back to the hospital if you want.

PATIENT: You think I'm being stupid.

KATIE: I think you're being irresponsible and ungrateful, which, from what I know about you, is perfectly in character.

PATIENT: No, but Katie, you have—

KATIE: Don't say my name! ...Don't come into my house and talk to me like you know me.

*(Pause)*

PATIENT: I *am* grateful. I don't know how to express it to you, what it is for me to be in this skin, to be relieved of the burdens that my body held. I know that your husband's body is a gift I don't deserve, I can see that you resent me inhabiting him, but, I don't want you to think I'm ungrateful. There are things I need to know about myself, and I won't find the answers sitting in the hospital, being a test subject. Do you understand?

KATIE: You don't owe me an explanation.

*(The* PATIENT *has pulled out some khakis, sneakers, a sweatshirt, a pair of boxer shorts.)*

PATIENT: Is there some place I could...

KATIE: Some place you could what?

PATIENT: Change? ...I'll just...go over here. *(He begins to exit, pulling off his shirt, then turns back, indicating his shoulder.)*

PATIENT: Hey, do you know what this scar is from?

*(*KATIE *looks at the* PATIENT, *at his shoulder. She turns front, trying to be as stony-faced as possible.)*

KATIE: It's from a sledding accident when he was a kid. He was thrown from...a toboggan, I think, and he landed on a broken a tree branch that was jutting out of the snow.

PATIENT: Such a wholesome injury.

*(*KATIE *does not respond, pause.)*

PATIENT: He was a good man, wasn't he?

KATIE: Yes.

*(The* PATIENT *moves off towards the kitchen, out of sight.* KATIE *begins to weep. He returns to find her crying. She is no longer looking at him. He comes up behind her, almost strokes her hair, but then places a hand on her shoulder. She jumps up.)*

KATIE: Jesus! DON'T TOUCH ME!

PATIENT: I'm sorry—

KATIE: IT'S SO FUCKING DISTURBING WHEN YOU TOUCH ME!

PATIENT: I'm sorry. It's disturbing for me, too.

KATIE: No. No, it's not. You don't— *(She cries.)*

PATIENT: I'm sorry.

*(The PATIENT takes a step towards KATIE. She backs away.)*

KATIE: No... No. *I'm* sorry. I'm sorry. I'm just so fucking hormonal and emotional and depressed.
   Oh. Okay. I'm going to go throw up now.

*(KATIE exits. The PATIENT looks after her. A door closes. He finds some socks and puts them and the sneakers on. She reenters, her face wet.)*

KATIE: Sorry.

PATIENT: Are you all right?

KATIE: Yeah. Morning sickness is a bitch, that's all.

*(KATIE sits. Pause)*

PATIENT: I didn't realize you were pregnant—
You would think someone would have told me that. Maybe they did. There's a lot, seemingly, that I don't remember from right before the surgery.

KATIE: There was nothing to tell you. I wasn't pregnant then.

PATIENT: *(With raised eyebrows)* Oh.

KATIE: Those procedures I was coming in for. We had some frozen sperm.

PATIENT: *Oh.*

KATIE: It was all set up. Beforehand. We'd been trying for a few years. It was just a matter of me deciding whether or not to go through with it. After.
   You're the first person I've told. Seems fitting. In a sick and bizarre kind of way. You found something that fits?

PATIENT: Yes. The pants are a bit loose. Iris told me I lost weight.

KATIE: You have.

PATIENT: Do you have his passport?

*(Pause)*

KATIE: Where are you going?

PATIENT: Home. To find the beginning. If I can.

*(Beat)*

KATIE: I'll go get it. *(She exits.)*

PATIENT: If you have a problem with it...

*(The PATIENT looks through more of Steve's stuff, pulling out more clothing, smelling some things. KATIE returns. She tosses an empty duffle bag at him.)*

KATIE: Here.

PATIENT: Thank you.

*(The PATIENT stuffs the clothes inside. KATIE hands him the passport.)*

KATIE: I don't think I'll tell Doctor Park you're leaving the country. He wouldn't forgive me.

PATIENT: You can tell him I'll be back before the pills run out.

KATIE: He wrote his cell number on all the bottles. You can tell him yourself.

PATIENT: Okay.

KATIE: Take care of yourself.

PATIENT: You too.

*(The PATIENT's eyes fall to KATIE's belly as the lights fade.)*

## Scene 13

*(Lights up on the Hammond residence. The place is a bit
cleaner. The boxes gone. The painted sheet music is on the
coffee table. The door bell rings. After a moment,* KATIE
*enters from the kitchen and goes to the door. She looks
through the peephole, then opens the door. It is* RAINA.*)*

RAINA: Is he here?

KATIE: Excuse me?

RAINA: Is he here?

KATIE: No. He's not here.

*(*RAINA *enters the house without invitation.)*

RAINA: Doctor Park said he came by here and you gave
him the medication.

KATIE: Yes.

RAINA: He gave me the medication, too, in case he came
to me. But he came here.

KATIE: He wanted some clothes.

RAINA: So you gave them to him.

KATIE: Yes. And then he left.

RAINA: He'll come back to me. I don't know what he's
told you, but he'll come back to me. He always does.

KATIE: Look, I don't know what you think/ happened—

RAINA: /Spare me, all right? I've heard it all before.
The "It's not what you think" and the "I don't know
what you're talking about," so spare me the lies and
the drama. He never promised me monogamy and I
never expected it. I wouldn't think to limit him, stifle
him in that way. But I think that you should know,

for your own sake, that he always comes back to me.
I'm the only one he trusts.

(*Pause.* RAINA *is so upset that she's visibly shaking,
on the verge of coming apart.*)

KATIE: Can I get you something to drink?

RAINA: Vodka, please, if you have it.

KATIE: I don't, I'm sorry. Root beer?

RAINA: Is it diet?

KATIE: No.

RAINA: I don't think—

KATIE: I could make you a root beer float. I was just
making one for myself.

RAINA: Oh. Well, that does sound good.

KATIE: Okay, make yourself comfortable.

(KATIE *exits.* RAINA *looks around the room. She looks at a
photo of Steve and the dog. She runs a finger along a surface
and finds it dusty.*)

RAINA: You have a lovely home.

KATIE: (*Off stage*) Thank you. I've been neglecting it
lately.

(RAINA *spies the painted sheet music. She picks it up.* KATIE
*enters with two root beer floats. She hands one to* RAINA.)

KATIE: Here you go.

RAINA: You know, this is worth at least five hundred
dollars.

KATIE: He gave it to me.

RAINA: I wasn't accusing you. I was just making you
aware of its value. You may want to flatten it. Steam
it a little and place it under a heavy book.

KATIE: Thanks for the advice.

(RAINA *takes a sip of her float.*)

RAINA: I don't remember the last time I had one of these.

KATIE: Two hours ago. That's the last time I had one.

RAINA: I imagine it's been a difficult couple of months for you.

KATIE: Hard to believe that's all it's been. Since the accident. Eight weeks? Nine?

RAINA: It's been almost six months since Claude had his leg amputated. Of course the dialysis started before that. It all sort of snowballed after his kidneys failed.

KATIE: You know, if I'd realized...the sort of artist... the sort of *man* he was....
    I don't think I would have signed all those papers.

RAINA: He's not the person the press made him out to be. A man overflowing with such genius can't be expected to behave like everyone else.

(*Beat*)

KATIE: So you don't mind that he's...been unfaithful?

RAINA: Did he sleep with you, in his state?

KATIE: That's not what I was saying. You implied that—

RAINA: Oh. No. It doesn't bother me. It's just sex. The other women can be tiresome, when they try to turn it into some kind of competition, which it's not. The real things, the truly intimate things like his fears and his art and his money. Those he shares only with me.

(KATIE *is not sure how to respond.*)

KATIE: Did the two of you...become romantically involved before or after you became his manager?

RAINA: "Romantically involved." That's sweet.
After. Shortly after.

KATIE: How long have you been his manager?

RAINA: Eighteen years. Why?

KATIE: Are you an artist yourself?

RAINA: Not a good one.

KATIE: Who told you *that*?

RAINA: There are certain things you have to
acknowledge on your own when no one else will
tell you.

KATIE: I guess it's nothing like golf. I mean, there's
definitely talent involved in golf, but if you practice
enough...

RAINA: I'm sure it's nothing like golf.

*(Pause)*

KATIE: Do you feel like a shadow or an influence?

RAINA: Excuse me?

KATIE: I just meant, as his manager, do you feel like his
fame overshadows you or do you feel like a part of it?

RAINA: The whole reason for doing it is to feel like a
part of it. Claude is one of the greatest artists of his time
and now, with this transplant, everyone has heard of
him. His immortality is guaranteed. For Christ's sake,
all van Gogh ever did was lop off his ear and look what
that did for his career.... And I have been there, every
step of the way, holding his hand, encouraging him,
pushing him. I am inextricably linked to that greatness.
I am aglow with it. I would never feel overshadowed
by it. Without me, Claude is merely a very talented
man, sitting in a dark studio, getting high off of paint
fumes and cognac. He's not capable of functioning

without me.
 Or, at least, he wasn't.

*(Pause)*

KATIE: Do you know anything about what caddies do?

RAINA: Aside from carrying the bag?

KATIE: Yes, aside from carting around the clubs.

RAINA: No, I can't say I have the slightest idea.

KATIE: Well, it's complicated and a little bit boring
to hear about—

RAINA: I'm sure.

KATIE: We give a lot of advice during a round.
Which clubs to use when. We learn the landscape
of each course, know the pin placements, which way
the greens break. And, then there's the psychological
aspect of the game. We sort of manage, handle the
player. Keep them focused. And for our services we
get a percentage of the winnings.

RAINA: How much?

KATIE: Traditionally ten percent.

RAINA: ...That's what I get.

KATIE: I used to play. Professionally.
 Steve and I were comparable golfers. I was...maybe
a little better.
 We tried to keep our relationship together, when we
were playing the respective tours, but...we never saw
one another. The schedules.
 I loved playing, but I didn't want to sacrifice our
relationship to it. ...And there's a lot more money to
be made on the men's tour, so I gave up my card and
became Steve's caddie.

RAINA: Did you like being a caddie?

KATIE: I think, to be a good caddie, it helps to be a good golfer. But to *like* being a caddie, you have to think you're not as good as the person you caddie for.

   That's why I asked you if you were an artist. I thought it might be the same.

RAINA: So will you go back and play yourself, now?

KATIE: Maybe in a couple of years.

RAINA: Why wait?

KATIE: Some medical reasons.

RAINA: Have I engaged in the golf discussion long enough that it is not offensive to change the subject?

KATIE: *(Laughing)* Sure. Far be it for me to bore you with the tedious details of my profession.

RAINA: Did he say where he's staying? I've looked everywhere for him, called everyone I know.

*(Beat)*

KATIE: I think he went to France.

RAINA: France.
   He can't go to France—I have his passport.

KATIE: He has Steve's passport.

RAINA: Does he.

KATIE: He said he wanted to go home. Remember his childhood.

RAINA: He doesn't want to remember that. He thinks it will make him feel complete again if he has all the pieces, but it's only going to hurt him. *(Pause)* He seems so much softer to me now, since the surgery. I don't want him to remember all the things that made him hard.

KATIE: For your sake or for his?

RAINA: For both of us.
We always had a difficult relationship.... I'd been
taking care of him for so long.... Not that my vigilance
did much to alter his behavior in the end.
   But, you know, he needed me. I was part of what kept
him going. I thought.... I don't know. I don't feel a
connection to him anymore. It's like we're strangers.
Since the surgery, Iris has been the one to keep him
going, and, well, it was very upsetting to see him
talking to you the other day. ... I always liked to believe
that love was a thing of the mind, but I don't think I can
believe that anymore.

KATIE: Why are you telling me this?

RAINA: Because there's no one else to tell. There is no
one else who would understand.

*(They take simultaneous sips of their floats as the lights fade.)*

## Scene 14

*(The Hammond living room recedes into the background and
the painted walls of the hospital room break away and are
spread across the stage. A classical melody being played on
a piano can be heard. The PATIENT enters carrying his
paintings on canvas. He looks at the wall, trying to decipher
it. He begins to place his older painting in the missing and
faded spots on the hospital wall. He moves them around as if
trying to solve a puzzle. One cohesive image begins to take
shape, though it is still abstract. It is an abstract view of the
inside of a grand piano from above. Inside the piano, hidden
beneath the strings, perhaps even obscured by dark gauze is
a little boy curled up in the fetal position. A large, ominous,
disembodied and haggard hand reaches into to the piano at
the boy.)*

*(The PATIENT stumbles backward and falls to his knees.
The lights go to black.)*

## Scene 15

*(The* PATIENT *sits against the stone wall of an old building. Music comes from above: single instruments reciting different pieces. He is in shock, slightly delirious and drunk. He hums along to something, gesturing vaguely, as if conducting.* RAINA *enters, seeing him she stops several feet away, unsure at first that it is him. He looks up and meets her eyes.)*

PATIENT: Raina.

RAINA: You ran away.

PATIENT: You came and found me.

*(Beat)*

RAINA: Of course.

PATIENT: Do you hear the music? All the different strains, the different composers weaving together. They're practicing so diligently.

RAINA: Have you been drinking?

PATIENT: Claude spent years of his life in this building. Thousands of hours at the keys....

*(*RAINA *kneels beside the* PATIENT, *touching his face.)*

RAINA: You have a fever. Have you been taking your medication?

PATIENT: You were right. He didn't want to remember. But I did. I wanted to know what happened to him that.... *(He looks at her, then looks away)* I didn't realize there was a difference. Between him and me. I didn't know who I was until I came here and saw that this is not my past. As clearly as I remember it, and as horrible as it was, it doesn't belong to me.
    That should make me feel better, but it doesn't.

I can't even look at you without seeing the things he's done in your face.

RAINA: Come on, Claude. You can't sit in the street like this. We need to get you to a doctor.

(RAINA *tries to take the* PATIENT'*s arm to help him up, but he pulls away.*)

PATIENT: I want to go home.

RAINA: All right.

PATIENT: I want to see my dog.

*(Beat)*

RAINA: You don't have a dog.

PATIENT: *(With a smile)* He recognizes me.

*(The lights fade.)*

### Scene 16

*(The lights come up on the Hammond living room. The* PATIENT *sits in Steve's chair. He wears the baseball cap* KATIE *gave him. He does not look well. Ambulance lights flicker through the windows. After a moment,* KATIE *enters with her golf bag slung over her shoulder. She glances at the him as she sets the clubs next to the door. There is much commotion outside: news crews, police, protestors.)*

KATIE: Hi.

PATIENT: Sorry about the people on the lawn.

KATIE: I thought the house was on fire when I drove up. But it's just you.

PATIENT: It's just me.

KATIE: How'd you get in?

PATIENT: The keys were in one of my pockets.

KATIE: I wondered where they went.

PATIENT: I asked Raina if we could stop by, so I could say hello before I went to the hospital.

KATIE: And then you locked yourself in.

PATIENT: Yes. I didn't want to go back there without seeing you.

KATIE: Raina is very upset.

PATIENT: Raina is perpetually upset.

KATIE: You don't look so good.

PATIENT: No.

KATIE: How was France?

PATIENT: Vivid.

KATIE: Did you remember what you needed to?

PATIENT: Too much.

*(Pause)*

PATIENT: This is a really nice house, you know that? A really nice house. A really nice, comfortable house. A person could feel at home in a place like this. In this chair, here. I can tell this is my chair because it fits me. Like the hat. *(Pause, then calmly)* It feels like the inside of my skull is on fire. Like my body is rejecting every thought I have. It's not so bad in here, though. When I sit here and look at you, it doesn't hurt.

KATIE: You should let them take you to the hospital.

PATIENT: How's the baby?

*(Beat. With wariness:)*

KATIE: Fine.

PATIENT: I never thought I'd have a child.

KATIE: You need to leave my house.

PATIENT: Did you know, when you started coming
to see me, I immediately felt connected to you. Even
though I didn't know who you were. The day you gave
me this hat, that was the first moment, when I realized,
and I said, "This is my hat." The words just popped out
of my mouth, and it was the first thing that I had said
or heard or seen since I woke up, that felt true.
   This place feels right. You do. Your skin. Your voice.
   When I'm with Raina, I can feel myself slipping back
into him. Into Claude. The mind games and the
manipulation. I feel that history and those habits start
to seep into this skin and it feels like...a desecration.
I know I could never be that person with you.
I wouldn't be capable of it.

KATIE: Look if you don't get up and go outside,
I'm going to let them in here and they will take you
out forcibly.

*(The* PATIENT *stands with effort, pauses a moment, then in
one quick movement he staggers towards* KATIE, *grabs her
by the shoulders and kisses her. She resists for a moment,
relents for several, then shoves him away.)*

KATIE: DON'T, don't do this to me.

PATIENT: Who do you think I am?

KATIE: I don't know.

PATIENT: I feel right here. This is my house, you are my
wife, that is my baby, and this is my hat! I know this.
*(He takes off his hat revealing an inflamed scar.)* This is my
hat!

KATIE: Okay. Let's go.

*(The lights go to black.)*

## Scene 17

*(The lights come up on the hospital room. It is evening and the lights are dim. The* PATIENT *lies in bed, feverish and ill. He holds his hat. A painting wrapped in brown paper leans against the foot of the bed.* RAINA *sits in a chair in the hall outside the room talking to* DOCTOR PARK.*)*

DOCTOR PARK: I'll ask him.

RAINA: Thank you, Doctor Park.

*(*DOCTOR PARK *enters the hospital room.* PATIENT *and* DOCTOR PARK *regard one another for a moment.)*

DOCTOR PARK: How are you feeling?

PATIENT: Not so great.

DOCTOR PARK: Still feel like your head's on fire?

PATIENT: Yeah.

DOCTOR PARK: The swelling isn't nearly what I thought it would be, but your fever.... Clearly the rest of your body has decided your brain is an alien object and is attacking it.

PATIENT: Rightly so.

DOCTOR PARK: You'll probably slip into a coma before you die.

PATIENT: Okay.

DOCTOR PARK: Was it worth it?

PATIENT: The surgery?

DOCTOR PARK: Your trip to France?

PATIENT: Well, if I hadn't gone I'd probably still be lying here wondering who I am, so yes, I guess it was worth it.

DOCTOR PARK: Worth dying for?

PATIENT: I think I would have died anyway.

DOCTOR PARK: But we don't know that now, do we?

PATIENT: You're angry with me.

DOCTOR PARK: I'm not angry. I'm disappointed....
And I'm angry.

PATIENT: Better to be honest about it.

DOCTOR PARK: I'm sorry it didn't work.

PATIENT: It was always a long shot.

DOCTOR PARK: Claude...

PATIENT: Is it so much to ask that you not call me
Claude.

DOCTOR PARK: I know it's late, but I'd like to have a
psychiatrist come talk to you.

PATIENT: Why? So you can have certification that I'm
crazy?

DOCTOR PARK: I'm concerned about this identity crisis
you're having.

PATIENT: I'm not having an identity crisis, I have
someone else's memories in my head!

(Beat)

DOCTOR PARK: I'd like to know if this is caused by
the surgery or by the rapid recovery of memories.
Perhaps it's a form of post-traumatic stress disorder
or maybe it's as simple as your psychological defense
mechanisms not functioning properly, post-surgery.

PATIENT: Doctor Park, I don't want to argue with some
stranger about who I am. I don't know why you can't
believe me.

DOCTOR PARK: So you're declining to meet with the psychiatrist.

PATIENT: Is that how you'd like to spend your last hours? Being a test subject? I won't submit to more poking and prodding, be it mental or physical.
You can test me when I'm dead.
  If you don't believe me, there's nothing else to say.

DOCTOR PARK: Fine.
  Ms van den Hoven is outside.
  She'd like to sit with you.

*(A beat. The* PATIENT *is torn.)*

PATIENT: No. I can't.

DOCTOR PARK: Don't you think it's better to have someone with you?

PATIENT: I can't. Not her.

DOCTOR PARK: All right.

PATIENT: Could you give her the painting that's by the foot of the bed?

DOCTOR PARK: I'll do that.

PATIENT: Tell her it's Claude's confession. Tell her I'm sorry.

*(*DOCTOR PARK *stares at him a moment, then nods and goes into the hallway, closing the door behind him.* RAINA *stands.)*

DOCTOR PARK: I'm sorry, he doesn't want any visitors. He asked me to give you this.

*(*RAINA *takes the package from him.* DOCTOR PARK *lingers for a moment, unable to convey the message. He exits.* RAINA *rips the paper to reveal a watercolor of herself, battered and bruised—lip fat, face cut, eye black and swollen. She is moved, upset. She sits. The lights fade.)*

## Scene 18

*(Lights come up on the hospital room. It is still night, the light is still dim.* IRIS *enters. She is wearing tight pants and a shimmery shirt. Her hair is very coiffed and she carries a trendy handbag. She is almost unrecognizable.)*

IRIS: *Bon soir, Monsieur.*

PATIENT: Iris?

IRIS: *Oui, Monsieur.*

PATIENT: I didn't recognize you.

IRIS: I know.

PATIENT: Doctor Park said you'd be in in the morning.

IRIS: He paged me. Told me you were back.

PATIENT: He must not think I'll make it 'til morning.

IRIS: He does not know, Monsieur.

PATIENT: Uncharted territory.

IRIS: *Oui.*

PATIENT: What were you doing? Dressed like that?

IRIS: I was out dancing.

PATIENT: What sort of dancing?

IRIS: I don't know, Monsieur. Just dancing. No partners. Lots of ass-shaking and sweating.

PATIENT: Like on a music video.

IRIS: I suppose.

PATIENT: Could you show me?

IRIS: No.

PATIENT: Not even one little shimmy?

IRIS: No!

PATIENT: Not even in my last hours?

IRIS: You might be faking.

PATIENT: You think so?

*(Beat)*

IRIS: No.

PATIENT: Will you miss me?

IRIS: I will be sorry that I have not known you long enough to miss you.

PATIENT: Well, that's something.... Do a lot of your patients die?

IRIS: Many.

PATIENT: Do you cry, ever?

IRIS: No. Transplant recipients get a second chance. Even if they die from it, it is more than most people get.

PATIENT: You know, I'm sort of relieved that I'm dying. These thoughts in my head. They might have driven me insane. Which would be worse, I think.
   Maybe he *was* insane.

IRIS: Who?

PATIENT: Claude. I don't feel like I know him that way. What he was. How he felt. I only know what he experienced, but it's not the same.

IRIS: You are not Claude?

PATIENT: Hasn't Doctor Park briefed you on my unstable mental condition?

IRIS: Who are you then?

PATIENT: Now *you* will call the psychiatrist.

IRIS: Are you Steve Hammond?

PATIENT: Doctor Park thinks I'm having an identity
crisis. I've tried to convince him otherwise, but he
doesn't want to listen.

IRIS: Of course not. He's a doctor. Doctors do not
believe the words that come out of a patient's mouth.
They only believe the sound of your heart beating in
your chest, the rasp of air as it passes into your lungs,
the read-outs from machines.... Hold my hand.

PATIENT: What?

IRIS: Hold my hand.

PATIENT: Why?

IRIS: Because it will tell me about you, and I will know,
and I will tell you, and then maybe you will know.

*(The* PATIENT *takes* IRIS's *hand, intertwining his fingers
with hers.)*

IRIS: You are a kind man. Confident. Self-assured.
Warm and open with others. Good with animals and
children. You are a gentle lover. There is a great deal of
strength in you, though right now you are a bit scared
and very weak. And your temperature and heart rate
are elevated.

PATIENT: Doesn't sound like the Claude I know.

(IRIS *does not respond)*

PATIENT: Is this some Haitian trick?

IRIS: No. Just what you can know from someone's touch.

PATIENT: Not a very scientific method.

IRIS: Oh, but it's very accurate, Monsieur. If one is
paying attention. It is almost impossible to lie with
the hands.

PATIENT: Maybe it's only residual Steve that you feel.
The lingering presence of a kinder man. And after time

these memories would harden him and make his touch...different. Maybe Claude's personality hasn't infiltrated this system enough for you to feel it.

IRIS: *(With soft humor)* You are afraid you have a monster lurking inside.

PATIENT: I know I do.

IRIS: You do not think the better man would triumph?

PATIENT: Maybe dying *is* the triumph.... You should go back to your dancing, Iris.

IRIS: Doctor Park said you sent Ms van den Hoven away.

PATIENT: Yes.

IRIS: What about Miss Katie?

PATIENT: She wouldn't come. She doesn't believe me, either. Rejection on all levels.

IRIS: Perhaps it is too much to ask a woman to sit at your deathbed twice.

PATIENT: Yes...

*(The PATIENT inhales sharply, in pain. IRIS takes his hand.)*

IRIS: I can get some morphine.

PATIENT: No. It is better to feel it. It will be over soon, anyway. *(Beat, he looks at her)* Have you ever had a patient die holding your hand before?

IRIS: Only a couple of times. Usually there is family.

PATIENT: Is it frightening? For you. To bear witness?

IRIS: It is a privilege. It is very sacred. *(Beat)* The first thing I ever saw die was a dog. It was back in Haiti, in my village. One of the few things I remember clearly. This dog. A sad, skinny dog. So thin you could count his ribs. He didn't belong to anyone in particular. I don't know what he lived on because everyone was too poor to be giving him food. We called him *"Dejeuner"*.

*(The* PATIENT *smiles.)*

IRIS: There was always talk about eating him, but no one ever did. When things were very bad, he seemed to know and stayed out of arm's reach. He was friendly, otherwise. But even I remember wondering what he would taste like.

I was picking flowers one day, and I found him lying in the tall grass by the edge of a field. He was breathing heavily. He looked so sad. I knew, somehow, that he was dying, though he didn't look hurt. I sat down next to him and pet him. He did not have nice fur, but I pretended I did not notice. His breathing was easier when I pet him. He seemed glad not to be alone. Not so frightened.

And then he let out his last breath and he was gone. There was nothing but a carcass beneath my hand. I put the flowers I had been picking on his belly and I left him there.

Strange that I remember him so clearly. A dog. I can't even remember my father's face.

*(Pause)*

PATIENT: Will you put flowers on my belly when I die?

*(This question takes* IRIS *completely by surprise, and moves her, almost to tears, though she gets it together quickly.)*

IRIS: I'd have to steal them from the other patients.

PATIENT: I'm sure they could spare a few.

IRIS: Would you rather I go off and gather flowers than sit with you?

PATIENT: No.

IRIS: Then I will stay, and you will hold my hand, and tell me who I am.

PATIENT: The great sorceress gives away her secrets.

IRIS: *Oui, Monsieur.*

*(The lights fade.)*

*(In the half-light the sounds of an E E G emerges: the heart beat is weak. Light comes up on* RAINA, *still waiting in the chair. On the opposite side of the stage, a soft light rises on* KATIE, *asleep in Steve's chair. The* PATIENT's *hand slips from* IRIS'. *Flatline.* KATIE *sits up with a gasp, then coughs violently, she looks around the room, searching. Lights out on* KATIE. *Meanwhile* IRIS *has crossed to* RAINA. IRIS *says something to* RAINA *that we cannot hear.* RAINA *nods, tears in her eyes.* IRIS *exits. Lights out on* RAINA. *The* ORDERLIES *have descended upon the* PATIENT, *slowly, respectfully undressing him and covering him with a sheet.)*

### Scene 19

*(Lights come up on the hospital room.* IRIS *is finishing up washing the* PATIENT. *A shroud covers the lower half of him.* DOCTOR PARK *enters. He grabs the* PATIENT's *chart and looks at it a moment before entering the room.)*

DOCTOR PARK: Time of death, 4:13 A M.

IRIS: Yes.

*(*DOCTOR PARK *sits in the chair next to the bed and regards its emptiness.)*

DOCTOR PARK: Were you here?

IRIS: Yes.

DOCTOR PARK: You're a braver soul than I.

*(Beat)*

IRIS: Thank you for paging me.

DOCTOR PARK: Of course. (*Pause, he sits next to her.*)
Has Ms van den Hoven been called?

IRIS: She was here—in the visitors lounge all night.
I told her.

DOCTOR PARK: Good. Thank you.

IRIS: You're welcome. (*Pause*) Will you do the autopsy
today?

DOCTOR PARK: I'd like to start but.... I don't think
there'll be time. The press conference....

(IRIS *nods.*)

IRIS: Hold his hands for me.

(*Beat.* IRIS *holds the* PATIENT'*s hands, waiting for* DOCTOR
PARK *to take then, daring him to refuse.*)

IRIS: Hold his hands.

(*After a hesitation,* DOCTOR PARK *holds the* PATIENT'*s
hands together as* IRIS *ties them. She covers his torso and
head with the shroud.* DOCTOR PARK *sits again.* IRIS *affixes
the toe tag to the* PATIENT'*s foot, wraps the shroud around
his feet and attaches another tag.* DOCTOR PARK *watches
her.*)

DOCTOR PARK: Are you going to transfer to maternity,
Iris?

(*Pause*)

IRIS: I don't know what purpose it would serve.
It would not change anything.

DOCTOR PARK: It would change me.
  You're my better half.

IRIS: I know.

(*Pause*)

DOCTOR PARK: I suppose I should go find my tie. Get ready for the camera crews. Think of something to say. Maybe we'll have better luck next time. *(He exits.)*

IRIS: Next time.

(IRIS *takes one last look at the shrouded body, crosses herself and exits also. Lights fade on the* PATIENT.*)*

## END OF PLAY

www.ingramcontent.com/pod-product-compliance
Lightning Source LLC
Chambersburg PA
CBHW052205090426

42741CB00010B/2413

* 9 7 8 0 8 8 1 4 5 3 7 3 7 *